The Book of Guinevere

Legendary Queen of Camelot

Andrea Hopkins

CRESCENT BOOKS
NEW YORK · AVENEL

Page 1: *An illustration from the beautifully illuminated fourteenth-century romance* Guiron le Courtois, *showing the young knight Guiron taking his leave of Arthur and Guinevere. (Bodleian Library, MS Douce 383 f.14)*

Page 2: *William Morris's portrayal of Guinevere in her chamber (sometimes considered to depict Iseult).*

Above: *Queen Guinevere at her husband's side watches as the knights of the Round Table take their leave, setting out on the Quest of the Holy Grail. Painting from 1849 by William Dyce, illustrating the virtue of Piety.*

This 1996 edition published by Crescent Books, distributed by Random House Value Publishing, Inc.
40 Engelhard Avenue
Avenel, New Jersey 07001

Random House
New York • Toronto • London • Sydney • Auckland

Produced by Saraband Inc., PO Box 0032, Rowayton, CT 06853-0032

A CIP catalog record for this book is available from the Library of Congress

ISBN 0-517-14269-4

10 9 8 7 6 5 4 3 2 1

Printed in China

Table of Contents

Introduction

Opposite: As a medieval heroine, Guinevere was the victim of conspiracies by wicked enemies, and often required rescuing. Here Lancelot triumphantly snatches a scantily clad queen from the grisly fate of being burned at the stake.

Most versions of the legend of King Arthur and the knights of the Round Table are very much focused on that noble king himself and his famous knights. His queen, Guinevere, is more elusive, less written about, and yet has been for centuries a central character playing a critical role in the rise and fall of the Round Table. Her character has been indelibly stamped by the moral censure of Tennyson's portrayal of her as weak and selfish. Tennyson added to the legend he had inherited from medieval sources a final interview between Arthur and Guinevere after the destruction of the Round Table. Guinevere, guilt-stricken, grovels on the floor at Arthur's feet, while he, depicted as a stern Victorian patriarch, delivers this crushing rebuke:

> I made them lay their hands in mine and swear
> To reverence their King, as if he were
> Their conscience, and their conscience as their King,
> To break the heathen and uphold the Christ,
> To ride abroad addressing human wrongs,
> To speak no slander, no, nor listen to it,
> To honour his own word as if his God's,
> To lead sweet lives in purest chastity,
> To love one maiden only, cleave to her
> And worship her by years of noble deeds,
> Until they won her; for indeed I knew
> Of no more subtle master under heaven
> Than is the maiden passion for a maid,
> Not only to keep down the base in man,
> But teach high thought, and amiable words
> And courtliness, and the desire of fame,
> And love of truth, and all that makes a man...
> And all this throve before I wedded thee,
> Believing "Lo, mine helpmate, one to feel
> My purpose and rejoicing in my joy."
> Then came thy shameful sin with Lancelot;
> Then came the sin of Tristan and Isolt;
> Then others, following these my mightiest knights,
> And drawing foul ensample from fair names,

Sinned also, til the loathesome opposite
Of all my heart had destined did obtain,
And all through thee!

TENNYSON, *Le Morte d'Arthur*

Right: *This stone in the Meigle Museum in Scotland is popularly believed to be Guinevere's grave monument. However, there is no historical evidence linking it to Guinevere, and Historic Scotland, who look after the stone, describe it simply as a "pictish symbol stone."*

Thus Guinevere has been stereotyped as a seductress and adulteress, so that little attention has been given to other aspects of her life and abilities. However, the picture of Guinevere that comes to us from medieval literature is much more varied and complex. This anthology of excerpts from mainly medieval but also later poems and prose about Queen Guinevere sheds fresh and interesting light upon her character.

The enduring mysteries and romance of Arthurian legend have continued to captivate and intrigue from the Middle Ages onwards. The enigma of Queen Guinevere, a beautiful and courageous queen or a disgraced adulteress, has received less attention than the achievements of King Arthur, the adventures of the noble Sir Lancelot and other knights, the magic of Merlin or the sorcery of Morgan le Fay. While the true location of Camelot and the actual power and influence of the Round Table have been studied and speculated on intensely for centuries, the character of Guinevere has remained more elusive. A key figure in the life of Camelot, this remarkable woman is seen variously as scholar, seductress, warrior and dignified gentle beauty by the countless artists and writers who have depicted her. Who, then, was Guinevere?

There is very little that is known as historical fact about King Arthur, and even less about his queen, Guinevere. No early source mentions her, but when she does begin to appear in medieval literature, certain features emerge strongly in her story, on which most of the medieval sources agree. These are: Guinevere is a very beautiful woman of noble or royal blood. Arthur marries her at the beginning of his reign. At some point during their marriage, she is abducted by a hostile noble or king and has to be rescued. Arthur, while fighting in France, leaves the government of the kingdom in her hands. While he is away, his nephew Mordred usurps the throne and attempts to marry Guinevere. This attempt is unsuccessful. Some versions of the story have Guinevere a co-conspirator in Mordred's plot, and perfectly willing to marry him; others show her very unwilling and desperately defending herself and the kingdom against him. In all sources, there is a strong tradition of Guinevere's adultery.

Later medieval society was strongly hierarchical and patriarchal. Certain details that appear in medieval retellings of this story can be interpreted in a way their authors were probably not aware of when they wrote. At this stage, it's very unlikely that we will ever recover the "very ancient British book" that Geoffrey of Monmouth claimed to have used, but he certainly had access to some source, whether it was really a book or Celtic oral tradition, which he worked into his history even though it was imperfectly understood by him.

Gildas, who wrote during the mid-sixth century, was the only contemporary historian to record this period of British history, when the

Opposite: Part of a stained glass window designed by William Morris, at Harden Grange, near Bingley, Yorkshire, showing Queen Guinevere.

Saxons were gradually conquering a post-Roman Britain weakened by internal power struggles. In his treatise On the Ruin of Britain, Gildas mentions that the seemingly inexorable Saxon westward advance across the island was halted for a considerable period by the actions of a notable war-leader ("dux bellorum") who unified the British against the invaders and fought a series of decisive battles against them, culminating in the famous victory of Mount Badon. The Saxons were so weakened after this that they encroached no further for fifty years. Archaeological evidence bears this story out.

Now there are certain curious things about this account. Frustratingly, Gildas does not name the war-leader, but there can be little doubt that, if Arthur ever existed at all, he was this leader. But why does Gildas refer to him as a war-leader, not a count or a king? Probably because he was neither a count nor a king, but someone who was simply a very able general and an outstanding leader. It can be reasonably speculated that this person seized power after the battles, and subsequently found it necessary to invent a royal background for himself to justify his claims. Hence the bizarrely inconvenient story of Arthur's supposed conception. In addition, Britain's was a society that, until Roman rule, had followed a matrilinear system of inheritance and descent. Royal power in particular was transmitted down the female line. So the self-made king could greatly improve his claim to sovereignty if he married a royal heiress. There is evidence in various medieval sources that Guinevere was such a person. Although Geoffrey says that she was of a Roman family, this is likely to have been Romano-British. The extraordinary thing about his account, and Wace's and Layamon's after him, is the coronation ceremony, in which Arthur and Guinevere each have their own procession, their own regalia and insignia, each are crowned in a separate church, and each follow this with their own feast in a separate palace. This implies that Guinevere had sovereignty in her own right and was not merely the consort of Arthur.

The mentions of Guinevere in Welsh literature give tantalizing glimpses of the persona that was rounded out much more fully in French, German and English medieval works. None of the surviving Welsh manuscripts is earlier than the eleventh century, though they undoubtedly contain much older material. In the collection known as the Triads, we find Guinevere mentioned twice. The Triads are basically a list of similar subjects or people, grouped in threes by category so as to remember them. Guinevere is first mentioned in Triad 56:

Three great Queens of Arthur's Court:
Gwenhwyfar daughter of Cywryd Gwent,
and Gwenhwyfar daughter of Gwythr ap Greidawl,
and Gwenhwyfar daughter of Gogfran the Giant.

This is mysterious and tiresome. Most people agree that it is very unlikely that this Triad means what it says, that there were three separate Guineveres who were all, either successively or at the same time, Arthur's queen. On the other hand, if it doesn't mean that, what does it mean? Various ingenious explanations have been forwarded, mostly along the lines that tripleness is a very significant quality and that this Triad links Guinevere with the three-personed goddess who appears in various guises in Celtic mythology. In Triad 80, there is a much less equivocal reference. Triad 80 is a list of the three unfaithful wives of the island of Britain, and at the end of it we find:

And one was more faithless than those three:
Gwenhwyfar, Arthur's wife, since she shamed
a better man than any of the others.

These two references, brief as they are, set the tone for the development of Guinevere's character in medieval literature. On the one hand, she was a great queen; on the other, she was an unfaithful wife. There was a huge variety of artistic response to this paradoxical person. Some authors, like the anonymous author of the French prose Lancelot, *writ-*

ten in the early 1200s, take a wholly approving view of Guinevere, though not shrinking in the least from showing her as the lover of Lancelot. In this work, moral judgement is not so much suspended as turned on its head, and Guinevere is described as a woman who is the model of propriety in conducting her love affairs! She is accused, ill-treated and victimized thanks to the plotting of her evil "twin" the False Guinevere; but the False Guinevere comes to a sticky end, and the author's approval of the real Guinevere never wavers. By contrast, the Guinevere who sexually harasses the hero of the Breton lay Lanval is a selfish, predatory, spiteful adulteress; far from being the faithful lover of Lancelot, she pounces on any knight who happens to catch her fancy and has no compunction in propositioning him in the most blatant terms. Worse, when she is thwarted, her wounded vanity makes her dangerously spiteful and she tries to have the unfortunate Lanval ruined and executed.

On balance, medieval authors tended to show Guinevere as a noble woman and a great queen, and in this book we shall be reading translated passages describing her early life, her marriage to Arthur, her everyday activities at court, her patronage of art and chivalry, her defence of Britain and herself against the wicked Mordred, as well as her love-affair with Sir Lancelot.

Guinevere the Young Queen and Bride

The young Guinevere has been portrayed in greater or lesser detail, variously as beautiful, eloquent, educated, rich and well-born; a prize Arthur coveted for the love she inspired in him, or perhaps for the dowry and position such a union would bestow. Accounts of their courtship and marriage reveal their authors' views of the young Guinevere and Arthur, and the political world they inhabited.

The earliest references to Guinevere in medieval literature do not say much directly about her background, social position or education. Geoffrey of Monmouth, in his History of the Kings of Britain, tells that she belonged to a noble Roman family, and had been brought up in the household of Cador, Duke of Cornwall. Wace, who translated Geoffrey into Anglo-Norman, and Layamon, who translated Wace into Anglo-Saxon, followed Geoffrey but added the detail that she was also related to Cador. However, they all give the same curious account of Arthur's and Guinevere's coronation ceremony, in which the king and queen are each crowned in a separate church with their own followers, and afterwards sit down each in their own palace to a separate feast:

And then, when he [Arthur] had restored the whole of his native land to its former dignity, he took a wife named Guenhumara, of a pre-eminently noble Roman family. She had been educated in the household of Cador, Duke of Cornwall, and she surpassed all the other women in the entire island in beauty.
[The coronation ceremony]…From another direction however the bishops and archbishops conducted the Queen, crowned with her own jewels, to the church of the young women dedicated to a religious life. And ahead of her walked the four queens of the four kings mentioned above, each carrying a white dove, as was the custom. All the married women who were there followed after her with the greatest rejoicing. Afterwards, when the procession had completed its course, there was so much organ music and so much singing in each of the two churches that because of its exceeding sweetness, the knights who were there did not know which of the churches to make for first. In crowds therefore they hurried, first to this one, now to that one, and even if the whole day had been spent in celebrating the rite, it would not have bred

tedium in any one of them. At length, the divine rites having been celebrated in both churches, the king and queen laid aside their crowns and, putting on lighter diadems, went forward to the banquet, he to his own palace with the men, she to hers with the women. For the Britons still preserved the ancient custom of Troy, that males should be served with other males, and women with other women, separately, to celebrate great feast days. When they had all been assigned to their seats accordingly as the rank of each one required, Kay the Seneschal, robed in ermine for the feast, and accompanied by a thousand noblemen who were all dressed in ermine too, served the great dishes of meat. And from another part, just as many who were wrapped in a dappled fur, following Bedivere the Butler handed out with him different kinds of drinks in all sorts of cups. In the queen's palace, meanwhile, innumerable servants dressed in different liveries were carrying out their duties, each busy with his own practice. If I were to continue to describe everything, I would create a story of enormous length.

GEOFFREY OF MONMOUTH,
History of the Kings of Britain

Above: *An exquisite miniature of the marriage of Arthur and Guinevere by the Flemish artist* Guillaume Vrelant, from Chroniques de Hainault, *about 1468. (Bibliothèque Royale Albert Ier, Brussels, MS 9243 f. 39 v)*

ace's Anglo-Norman verse rendering of Geoffrey's history, the Roman de Brut, *follows him closely in substance but adds in significant detail:*

When Arthur had restored his realm to peace, righted all wrongs, and reinstated the ancient borders of the kingdom, he took as wife a certain lovely and noble maiden named Guinevere, and made her his queen. This maiden was very beautiful, with courteous and stately manners, she was descended from a noble Roman family. Duke Cador of Cornwall had for a long time nobly nurtured this lady in his earldom. Through his mother, the earl was also of Roman blood, and so the maiden was his cousin. This maiden was wonderfully exquisite and fine in her clothes and figure; she bore herself like a queen, and she was also eloquent and elegant in speech. Arthur loved her dearly, for his love was wonderfully set upon this maiden; yet they never had a child together, nor between them could they beget an heir...

Right: *In this rather saccharine painting by Herbert James Draper, Guinevere catches sight of Lancelot for the first time during the preparations for her wedding to Arthur.*

Then the history tells of this occasion [the coronation], that when the morning was come of the day of the high feast, a fair procession of archbishops, bishops, and abbots went to the king's palace, to place the crown upon Arthur's head, and lead him into the church…

So that the queen should not be overshadowed by her husband's state, the crown was set on her head in another fashion. For her part she had invited to her court the great ladies of the country, ladies that were the woves of her friends. Together with these had assembled the ladies of her kindred, those whom she liked the most, and many fair and gentle maidens whom she wished to have close to her at the feast. The presence of this gay company of ladies made the feast even richer, when the queen was crowned in her chamber, and brought to that convent of holy

nuns for the conclusion of the rite. The crowd was so dense that the queen could scarcely make her way through the streets of the city. Four ladies preceded their lady, bearing four white doves in their hands. These ladies were the wives of those lords who carried the golden swords before the king. A fair company of maidens followed after the queen, making marvellous joy and delight. This fair fellowship of ladies came from the noblest of the realm; they were wondrously beautiful, and wore rich mantles above their silken dresses. Everyone gazed on them with pleasure, for each was as beautiful as her companions…When the ceremony drew to its pre-ordained close, and the last words were sung, the king took off the crown he had worn to the church, and took another crown that was lighter to wear, and so did the queen. They laid aside their heavy robes and ornaments of state, and dressed themselves in less fatiguing clothes. The king then went from St Aaron's Church and returned to his palace for the feast. The queen, also, returned to her own palace, accompanied by the fair fellowship of ladies, all marvellously joyful…the queen had so many servants at her command, that I cannot tell you the number. She and her company of ladies were properly and respectfully served.

WACE, *Roman de Brut*

Wace is also the first Arthurian writer to mention the Round Table, which became such an integral part of the later medieval legends. Wace introduces the Round Table as a device invented by Arthur to prevent quarrels about precedence among his proud knights:

Because of these noble barons that Arthur had, each one of whom strove to be the best, and none of whom would think himself a lesser man than the others, Arthur made the Round Table, of which so many stories are told in Britain. This table was fashioned so that every knight and vassal had an equal place; when they sat down to eat they were served equally, and no man could boast that he was in a higher place than his peers. No one was considered a stranger there; no one was treated any more or less courteously because he was a Scot, a Breton, an Angevin, a Fleming, a Burgundian or a Loherin.

WACE, *Roman de Brut*

Layamon's Anglo-Saxon alliterative verse translation of Wace adds yet more details about a fight among the knights that demonstrated the need for the table, and exactly how it was

Opposite: *The young Guinevere in an idyllic pastoral landscape— Eleanor F. Brockdale's vision of Guinevere in her illustrations to Tennyson's Idylls of the King.*

constructed. Malory, however, preserves a distinct tradition that the Round Table belonged to Guinevere's father King Leodegraunce of Cameliard and was given to Arthur with Guinevere as her dowry. He follows his French source in having Merlin warn Arthur against marrying Guinevere because of the strife that will be caused by her love for Lancelot, but Arthur chooses not to listen. In Malory's version of events, it seems that Arthur's motivation to marry her is, at least in part, to retrieve the Round Table, which his own father Uther Pendragon had previously given to Leodegraunce:

So it fell on a time King Arthur said unto Merlin, "My barons will let me have no rest, but needs I must take a wife, and I will none take but by thy counsel and by thine advice."

"It is well done," said Merlin, "that you take a wife, for a man of your bounty and noblesse should not be without a wife. Now is there any that you love more than another?"

"Yea," said King Arthur, "I love Guinevere the king's daughter, Leodegraunce of the land of Cameliard, who holdeth in his house the Table Round, that you told he had from my father Uther. And this damosel is the most valiant and fairest lady that I know living, or yet that ever I could find."

"Sir," said Merlin, "as of her beauty and fairness she is one of the fairest alive, but, if you loved her not so well as you do, I should find you a damosel of beauty and of goodness that should like you and please you, if your heart were not set; but where as a man's heart is set, he will be loth to turn back."

"That is truth," said King Arthur. But Merlin warned the king covertly that Guinevere was not wholesome for him to take to wife, for he warned him that Lancelot should love her, and she him again; and so he turned his tale to the adventures of the Sangreal. Then Merlin desired of the king for to have men with him that should enquire of Guinevere, and so the king granted him, and Merlin went forth unto King Leodegraunce of Cameliard, and told him of the desire of the king that he would have unto his wife Guinevere his daughter.

"That is to me," said King Leodegraunce, "the best tidings that ever I heard, that so worthy a king of prowess and noblesse will wed my daughter. And as for my lands, I will give him, if I knew it might please him—but he hath lands enough, he needs no more, but I shall send him a gift shall please him much more, for I shall give him the Table Round, which Uther Pendragon gave me, and when it is full complete, there is an hundred knights and fifty. And as for an hundred good knights I have myself, but I lack fifty, for so many have been slain in my days."

The stateliest of her altar-shrines, the King
That morn was married, while in stainless white,
The fair beginners of a nobler time,
And glorying in their vows and him, his knights
Stood round him, and rejoicing in his joy.
Far shone the fields of May thro' open door,
The sacred altar blossom'd white with May,
The Sun of May descended on their King,
They gazed on all earth's beauty in their Queen,
Roll'd incense, and there past along the hymns
A voice as of the waters, while the two
Sware at the shrine of Christ a deathless love:
And Arthur said, "Behold, thy doom in mine.
Let chance what will, I love thee to the death!"
To whom the Queen replied with drooping eyes,
"King and my lord, I love thee to the death!"
And holy Dubric spread his hands and spake,
"Reign ye, and live and love, and make the world
Other, and may thy Queen be one with thee,
And all this Order of thy Table Round
Fulfil the boundless purpose of their King!"

TENNYSON, "THE COMING OF ARTHUR"
FROM *Idylls of the King*

Left: The now legless painted Round Table that hangs on the west wall of the great hall of Winchester Castle. Malory had seen this table and explained that Camelot was the old name for Winchester. The timbers for the table were felled in about 1250–55, and its painting dates from 1513.

Guinevere the Victim of Abduction

O ne of the oldest and most enduring episodes concerning Guinevere in the Arthurian legend tells that she was abducted by an adversary hostile to Arthur, taken away to his castle, and subsequently rescued and returned to Arthur. Depending on the author, the portrayal of Guinevere in this tale of abduction varys from that of helpless, innocent victim or billiant strategist outwitting her captor to scheming co-conspirator betraying her kingdom.

The first medieval text to mention Guinevere at all is the Life of St. Gildas written by one Caradoc, a monk of the abbey of Llancarfan in about 1130. He tells how "King Melwas" of the Summer Country carries Guinevere off to his fortress near Glastonbury:

Gildas came to Glastonbury, where King Melwas ruled the Summer Country…Glastonbury used to be called the Isle of Glass in the British language. It was besieged by Arthur the tyrant with a huge host, because of his wife Guennuvar, who had been raped and carried off by the aforementioned wicked king, who brought her there because it was an impregnable position, surrounded by river, marsh, and reeds. The angry king had sought the queen for a whole year, and at length heard that she was there. At this, he raised the armies of the whole of Devon and Cornwall, and the adversaries prepared for battle. On seeing this, the Abbot of Glastonbury and his priests, and Gildas the Wise sallied out between the two armies, and in the name of peace advised their king Melwas to return the lady he had abducted. So she was returned, as she should have been, in peace and good will.

CARADOC OF LLANCARFAN, *Life of St. Gildas*

T his is the first Arthurian text to link King Arthur with Glastonbury, and it introduces several intriguing features which indicate a shared tradition with the classic version of Guinevere's abduction, the Lancelot of Chrétien de Troyes, written probably in the 1160s or 1170s. Caradoc's Melwas is probably the same name as Meleagant; though in Chrétien's story, he is not a king, he is a king's son. Melwas takes Guinevere to his own land, called "Gorre," which exhibits several features of a Celtic otherworldly kingdom—it is difficult to get into, can only be entered by crossing water, and, surrounded by water and defended by magical illusions, impossible to leave without its ruler's permission. Similarly, though Caradoc does his best to ground his story in a real context by explaining that Melwas's retreat was at Glastonbury (and, by implication, that the mysterious-sounding Summer Country is Somerset), Melwas has the aura of a Celtic legendary character.

At the opening of Chrétien's Lancelot, Meleagant appears very much as the unknown, mysterious, otherworldly champion; but Chrétien is not really interested in the details of Guinevere's abduction. He is much more interested in the psychological drama to be enacted later between Lancelot, Guinevere, Meleagant (who quickly dwindles into a petulant, unprincipled weakling, repeatedly upbraided for his conduct by his noble father) and Bagdemagus. This is the first literary appearance of Lancelot, and the first and one of the most explicit accounts of the adulterous love affair between Lancelot and Guinevere. Interestingly, Lancelot appears in another romance as the defender and would-be rescuer of Guinevere, in the Lanzelet of Ulrich von Zatzikhoven, written about 1205. In this version there is no suggestion that Lancelot is the queen's lover, and in fact her rescue from her abductor (here called King Valerin) is brought about by the interference of the wizard Malduc rather than by Lancelot fighting as her champion.

Another very early account of Guinevere's abduction is to be found depicted in a stone carving on an archivolt over the north door at Modena Cathedral. The carving shows a moated castle in which a lady is being held prisoner by a man and all the characters are identified by names carved above them—these two are "Winlogee" and "Mardoc." To the left of the castle a man called "Burmaltus" defends it with an axe against three mounted knights, two of whom are named as "Isdernus" and

Below: A wonderful medieval depiction of Lancelot rescuing the abducted Guinevere. He crosses the sword bridge (note the blood pouring from his hands and knees), fights the lions, and jousts against the wicked Meleagant, watched by Guinevere and Bagdemagus. This is the opening page of a manuscript dated 1344. (Bibliothèque Nationale, Paris, MS Fr. 122 f. 1)

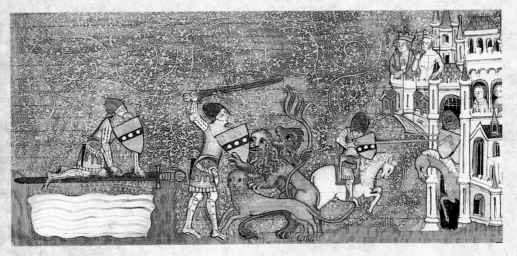

"*Artus de Bretania.*" *To the right of the castle, a knight named "Carrado" is riding out of the gate to attack "Galvagin," behind whom ride "Galvarium and "Che." Though this does not fit with any known literary source, some characters are recognizable as Arthur, Yder, Guinevere, Marduc, Carrados, Gawain and Kay. The significance of this carving is its early date—between 1120 and 1140—and its distance, in northern Italy, from the likely home of the early oral traditions about Arthur and Guinevere. It shows that this seminal episode was very widely known some time before the earliest surviving written source.*

Neither this carving nor Caradoc of Llancarfan give any indication of whether Guinevere was a willing victim of abduction (though Caradoc implies that she had been raped by Melwas). Geoffrey of Monmouth records that Guinevere went with Mordred of her own accord:

When it was full summer, he was preparing to seek the way to Rome, and had begun to climb the mountains, when he was informed that his own nephew Mordred, in whose charge he had left Britain, through outrageous treachery had usurped his crown, and had coupled together in wicked lust with Queen Guinevere, who had violated the vows of her former marriage. But on this subject, mighty lord, Geoffrey of Monmouth will be silent...

GEOFFREY OF MONMOUTH,
History of the Kings of Britain

Right: *Another, slightly less action-packed medieval manuscript illustration. Lancelot crosses the sword bridge, while Guinevere and Bagdemagus watch from the tower on the left; on the right King Bagdemagus greets the victorious Lancelot. (Pierpont Morgan Library, MS 806 f. 166)*

ace follows this account closely, but Layamon elaborates considerably with the first literary treatment of Arthur's ominous dream about the wreck of his fortunes the very night before he learns of his nephew's and his wife's treachery:

Then Mordred came in there with a huge army; he bore in his hand a strong battle-axe. He began to hew mightily, and split in pieces the posts that held up the hall. And there too I saw Wenhaver, dearest of women to me; she pulled down the greater part of the hall roof with her hands. The hall began to collapse, and I fell to the ground, so that my right arm was broken. Then Mordred said, "Take that!", the hall fell down, and Gawain began to fall, and tumbled to the ground; both his arms were broken. And I grasped my beloved sword in my left hand, and smote off Mordred's head, so that it rolled on the ground. And I hacked the queen all to pieces with my trusty sword; and after that I threw her down in a black pit...Then I woke up; at once I began to tremble, then I began to shudder as if I were burning with fever. And I have been thinking about this dream of mine all night, for I am sure that all my happiness is destroyed; I must endure only sorrow now for as long as I live. Alas! That I do not have Wenhaver my queen here with me!

LAYAMON, *Brut*

knight consoles him: if his dream is an omen of the truth, then he will be able to avenge himself by force of arms. Touchingly, Arthur replies, "As long as eternity, I shall never believe that Mordred my kinsman would ever betray me even for my kingdom, or that Wenhaver my queen would weaken in resolve; that would never start to happen, not for any man on earth." The knight then tells him the awful truth.

Malory, however, following the French prose Mort Artu, has Mordred abducting Guinevere very definitely against her will. In his story, Mordred convenes a parliament of lords and shows them letters he had forged, ostensibly from overseas, bearing news of Arthur's death in battle. He persuades the lords to choose him as king and announces his intention to marry Guinevere, who is appalled at the news but feigns willing acceptance. She then devises a clever plan to escape her captor:

Then she desired of Sir Mordred for to go to London, to buy all manner of things that belonged unto the wedding. And because of her fair speech Sir Mordred trusted her well enough, and gave her leave to go. And so when she came to London she took the Tower of London, and suddenly in all haste possible she stuffed it with all manner of victual, and well garnished it with men, and so kept it.

Then when Sir Mordred wist and understood how he was beguiled, he was passing wroth out of measure. And a short tale for to make, he went and laid a mighty siege about the Tower of London, and made many great assaults thereat, and threw many great engines unto them, and shot great guns....Then [he] sought

rtus
de vr
la cu
noul
que
preu
tant
com
a œl
u t

on apele la renteæ

l t court fu a carduel

a pres mangier pun

l rcheualier cauvpele

l au damer ler apele

I suppose, or because we didn't deign to! Upon my word, sir, we certainly did not do so, but only because we did not see my lady until after you had stood up."

"Really, Kay," said the queen, "you're so full of venom that in my opinion, if you didn't spit it out, you'd burst. You are rude and malicious to insult our friends thus."

"Lady!" replied Kay, "if we are not to gain by your company, at least take care that we are not worse off for it! I don't think I have said anything that should be set down as wicked on my account, and so I beg you, keep quiet about it. It's neither courteous nor wise to maintain an argument on such a trivial subject."

…At these words Calogrenant responded thus: "Sir! I am not greatly concerned about the argument; it means little to me, and it doesn't matter. If you have offended me, I shall never be harmed by it: you have often insulted braver and wiser men than I, sir Kay; it's something you're in the habit of doing. Just as a dung-heap must always stink, a gadfly must always sting, a bee must buzz, and so a spiteful bore will always distress and annoy others. But, if my lady will excuse me, I will tell no more today, and I pray her to say no more about it, and not to command me to do anything disagreeable to me."

"Lady, everyone who is here," said Sir Kay, "would be grateful to you; for they would willingly hear [the rest of the story]; you wouldn't be doing it for my sake! But for the faith you owe the king, your lord and mine, command him [to continue], if you want to do well."

"Calogrenant," said the queen, "do not concern yourself about the attack by my lord Kay the Seneschal. He is so much in the habit of speaking evil that one cannot even chastise him for it. I want to command you and request you not to feel anger in your heart because of it, nor on his account to refrain from telling us things that we would very much like to hear."

*C*alogrenant relates his tale, in which he is defeated by the Knight of the Fountain in a humiliating adventure. When the story is finished, his cousin, Yvain, vows to avenge the disgrace, to which Kay responds spitefully and once more attracts the queen's sharp disapproval:

"The devil, Sir Kay, are you out of your mind?" said the queen. "Can your tongue never stop wagging? Cursed be that tongue of yours, which is so packed with gall! Truly, your tongue must hate you; for it says the worst thing that it knows how to everyone, whoever they may be. Such a tongue, that never tires of speaking

Or dist li contes que mout
furent li compaignon
de la table reonde lie qui
furent acorde amon singnior ca

evil, should be accursed! Your tongue behaves itself in such a way that it makes you hated by everyone. It could not betray you more effectively. In fact, I would accuse it of treason if it belonged to me. A man who cannot control his mouth should be tied in front of the choir-screen at church, like a madman."

…While they were talking like this, the king came out of his chamber, where he had been for a long while; for he had slept until this moment. And the barons, when they saw him, all leapt to their feet to meet him, and he made them all sit down again. He seated himself beside the queen, and the queen at once told him the adventures of Calogrenant word for word, for she knew how to tell a story well and skilfully.

CHRÉTIEN DE TROYES, *Yvain*

Opposite: *In this manuscript in the Bibliothèque Nationale in Paris, Guinevere holds a little dog, the perfect royal consort by her husband's side, while Arthur discusses falconry with King Ban. (MS Fr. 95 f.291)*

Chrétien labours this comparatively trivial incident at length—as, in his story, Kay had accused the queen of doing. But he provides a great deal of information about Guinevere and her position at court. In the first place, this is a Guinevere who clearly enjoys full conjugal relations with her husband, withdrawing with him to their bedchamber even in the middle of a banquet and exhausting him so that he falls asleep, much to the scandal of some of the court. She is clearly a beautiful, confident, sexually attractive woman, very much in command of herself and her courtiers. When she hears Kay launch one of his bullying, sarcastic attacks on a very junior knight, she immediately defends him with pungent comments. She is not only articulate but also very witty, and one can imagine how much the medieval readers of this romance would enjoy such sophisticated repartee. The court is clearly a place where polite conventions are strictly honoured, as evidenced by the fuss Kay creates when Calogrenant is the only knight quick enough to stand up when Guinevere enters the room. And Guinevere enjoys the perfect confidence of the king: she is the one to put him fully in the picture when he finally emerges from his bedroom.

In another romance, Chrétien presents us once more with delicious glimpse of court life. Despite their less-than-cordial relationship in Yvain, at the beginning of Lancelot, King Arthur employs Guinevere as the capable go-between to mediate between himself and Sir Kay, who is threatening to leave him. But the situation is loaded with the potential for Chrétien's favourite kind of irony. This is his version of the story of Guinevere's abduction. The wicked knight who loves her, Meleagant, has just issued a bold challenge to the court: let the best knight follow him into the forest, leading Guinevere with him, and fight with him for the right to take her; if the challenge is refused, Arthur's court will lose its reputation for knightly pre-eminence. In

Opposite: *A very fine early twentieth-century line drawing by H. Ford captioned: "Arthur and Guinevere Kiss Before All the People"—another illustration to a retelling of Malory's* Le Morte d'Arthur.

the ensuing confusion, Kay suddenly threatens to leave the court and the service of the king. Arthur begs him to stay, but he refuses, and will not reveal the reason for his decision. Arthur turns to Guinevere:

"My lady," he said, "do you know what the seneschal has asked me? He asks leave to depart and says that he will remain in my court no longer; I don't know why. But what he refuses to do for me, he will quickly do at your request; go to him, my dear lady; since he will not agree to stay for my sake, beg him to stay for yours, and even, if necessary, cast yourself at his feet, for I shall never be happy if I lose his company."... she found [Kay] with the others, and when she came before him, she said: "Kay, I hope you realise that I am very deeply distressed by the news I have heard spoken about you. I've been told, and it hurts me, that you mean to leave the king. How has this come about? What is in your mind? You are neither so prudent nor so courteous as you used to be. I want to beseech you to remain: stay with us, Kay, I beg you."

"Lady," said Kay, "I thank you; but I cannot remain another moment." Then the queen once again implored him, and all the knights together with her; but Kay told her that she would tire herself out in useless effort. Then the queen, high as she was, fell at his feet. Kay begged her to rise; but she refused; she said she would never stand up again unless he granted her wish. Then Kay promised he would remain, provided that the king and she would agree to grant him in advance whatever he requested.

"Kay," she said, "whatever it may be, both he and I will grant it; now come, and let us tell him that you will remain on this condition." Kay then went with the queen; they appeared before the king. "Sire," said the queen, "I have retained Kay, but it was very hard work, and I have only achieved it by promising that you will perform whatever he asks." The king gave a sigh of happiness, and said that he would do Kay's will, whatever he might ask.

"Sire," said Kay, "now know the gift that I desire, and the gift that you have promised me; I hold myself very fortunate that I shall have it, thank you. You have agreed to entrust the queen to me; we shall go after the knight who waits for us in the forest."

The king was sorry, but he entrusted Kay with the queen, for never on any account was he false to his word; but it made him angry and miserable, which very soon appeared in his face. The queen was also very distressed by it, and everyone in the household said that it was arrogant, presumptuous, and absurd of Kay to make such a request. And the king took the queen by the hand and said, "My lady, you must go with Kay, without resistance."

And Kay said: "Now entrust her to me, and have no fear about anything, for I shall bring her back again quite safe and unhurt."

The king reluctantly entrusts Guinevere to Sir Kay, who leads the downcast queen away on a pony. The court laments her departure fearing that it will be the last they see of her.

CHRÉTIEN DE TROYES, *Lancelot*

I n Thomas Malory's version of this incident, Meleagant abducts Guinevere as she is out "Maying" with ten unarmed knights — a rare description of the queen's non-amorous activities:

So it befell in the month of May, Queen Guinevere called unto her knights of the Table Round; and she gave them warning that early upon the morrow she would ride on Maying into woods and fields about Westminster: "And I warn you that there be none of you but he be well horsed, and that ye all be clothed in green, either in silk or in cloth; and I shall bring with me ten ladies, and every knight shall have a lady behind him, and every knight shall have a squire and two yeomen, and I will that you all be well horsed."

So they made them ready in the freshest manner…And so upon the morn they took their horses with the queen, and rode Maying in woods and meadows as it pleased them, in great joy and delights; for the queen had intended to have been again with King Arthur at the furthest by ten of the clock, and so was that time her purpose…And at that time was such a custom, the queen rode never without a great fellowship of men of arms about her, and they were many good knights, and the most part were young men that would have worship; and they were called the Queen's Knights, and never in no battle, tournament, nor jousts, they bare none of them no manner of knowledging of their own arms, but plain white shields, and thereby they were called the Queen's Knights.

MALORY, *Le Morte d'Arthur*

I n these short passages we observe Guinevere apart from the drama of her doomed love affair with Lancelot. The portrait we have is approving; this is a leader, an arbiter of taste and fashion, an active, energetic, able woman, accustomed to command, valuing courtesy, setting high standards of courtly behaviour for her knights and followers.

Opposite: *Guinevere as a young girl in the "golden days" before she was troubled by the sin and guilt of her adulterous love for Lancelot. The Tennysonian idea of the Queen, as interpreted by Eleanor F. Brockdale.*

Guinevere the Lover

Of all the tales in Arthurian legend featuring Guinevere, one of the best known is the story of her love-affair with Sir Lancelot. The portrayal of her as an adulteress is one with which most are familiar and it seems from references to Guinevere in Welsh poetry that she was infamous as an unfaithful wife from an early date. The tone of these references is definitely one of strong disapproval, but the peculiar ethos of courtly love turned this moral censure of an adulteress on its head, and made Guinevere the model of polished behaviour for a married woman bestowing her favours on a bachelor knight.

In Chrétien de Troyes's Lancelot, also known as The Knight of the Cart, Guinevere appears as a very demanding, though also very rewarding, mistress. The poem tells the story of Guinevere's abduction by the wicked Meleagant and rescue by Lancelot, but it also shows how Lancelot is taught a lesson in proper loverly submission to his mistress. Chrétien tells us in his introduction that the subject matter and the meaning of the poem were given to him by Marie, Countess of Champagne, and it may be that he was not totally happy with the content, as he left the poem to be finished by someone else.

Chrétien first shows us that Lancelot (who, for the first part of the poem, is not named) is so passionately in love with Queen Guinevere that he worships her almost as a deity, and is quite beyond the reach of reason. At one point, Lancelot and Gawain are lodging together in their pursuit of the queen. Lancelot sees from his window a procession of people including a tall knight leading a beautiful lady on horseback:

The knight at the window recognised that it was the Queen. As long as she remained in his sight, he continued to gaze at her most attentively, and with delight. But when he could see her no longer, he wanted to fling himself out of the window and shatter his body on the ground below. He was already halfway out of the window when my lord Sir Gawain spotted him and pulled him back in. "Sir, for heaven's sake, calm yourself!" he said. "For the love of God, never think of doing such an insane thing again! You are very wrong to hate your own life thus."

A little later on, Lancelot finds a comb by the roadside with several golden hairs caught in its teeth. Informed that the comb and the hairs belonged to Queen Guinevere, he seizes the hairs:

…he began to adore the hairs; a hundred thousand times he touched them to his eyes, his mouth, his forehead, and his cheeks. His joy was made manifest in every way, and he thought himself rich and happy indeed. He placed the hairs in his breast, close to his heart, between the shirt and the skin. He would not exchange them for a cartload of emeralds and carbuncles…

CHRÉTIEN DE TROYES, *Lancelot*

Above: *Queen Guinevere on horseback. One of Aubrey Beardsley's wonderfully baroque line drawings, from an illustrated edition of Malory's Le Morte d'Arthur, 1893.*

ancelot also undergoes considerable suffering during his rescue attempt. Early on in his pursuit of the queen and her kidnapper, Lancelot is compelled to ride in a cart, something which, Chrétien assures us, was considered very disgraceful in those days, as only criminals ever rode in carts on their way to be executed. Lancelot hesitates before entering the cart, reluctant to bring shame on his rescue attempt, but as this is the only way he can learn where the queen has been taken, he gets in. He then suffers constant shame as he is ridiculed by everyone he meets as "the knight of the cart," and is subjected to all kinds of danger and pain, including crawling on his bare hands and knees over a bridge composed only of the blade of a sword, before doing battle with the wicked Meleagant for the queen's freedom.

Lancelot defeats Meleagant, then disarms himself and hurries to present himself to the queen. She refuses to speak to him or even look at him. Not surprisingly, Lancelot is dumbfounded; sorrowfully leaving the court, he concludes that she now hates him because he disgraced himself by riding in the cart. Later in the poem, after fearing one another dead, the lovers are reconciled, and Lancelot then learns that Guinevere's former cold behaviour was a punishment, not for riding in the cart, but for hesitating to get into it. He had put his knightly reputation before her safety for the briefest of moments—not good enough by the queen's exacting standards!

In the final section of the romance (the part not written by Chrétien) Lancelot demonstrates his absolute submission to Guinevere's will. He attends a tournament in disguise and, at first, fights like a prodigy—as a knight should who wants to impress his beloved. The queen recognizes him and sends him a message that he is to "do his worst." Obediently, Lancelot starts to miss his opponents, and then runs away from them, until all the other knights despise him for a coward. All day, and all the following day Lancelot obeys the queen's instruction—a complete inversion of the normal striving to win in order to please one's lady and bring her honour. It is also a much keener test of Lancelot's love for Guinevere, since it contradicts his self-love. Once Guinevere is satisfied that Lancelot is sufficiently humble and obedient, and has learned his lesson, she tells him to do his best, whereupon he fights so magnificently that he wins the tournament prize.

However, Guinevere is not always severe on Lancelot or maintaining a distance. After they have been reconciled with each other, Lancelot asks if he can speak to her in private. She is being kept a virtual prisoner in the castle of King Bagdemagus—mainly for her own protection, to keep Bagdemagus's son Meleagant away from her—and she warns Lancelot that they cannot be together physically. The door of her chamber is kept locked and guarded night and day, she has

Below: *This famous miniature shows Lancelot and Guinevere's first kiss. The scene is from the French prose* Roman de Lancelot du Lac. *On the left, Lancelot's friend Galehot allows the lovers to kiss unobserved (he thinks) by the nearby courtiers. On the right, Guinevere's ladies-in-waiting converse with a seneschal. One of them, the beady-eyed Lady of Malohaut, has seen the kiss and becomes Guinevere's confidante. (Pierpont Morgan Library, MS 805 f. 67)*

the badly wounded Sir Kay sleeping in her room, and the window is protected by thick iron bars. Nevertheless, she invites Lancelot to speak with her at the window later that night:

When Lancelot perceived the Queen leaning towards the window at the massive iron grille, he greeted her in a low voice. The Queen returned his greeting, for she greatly desired him, as he did her. In their words was nothing base or disagreeable, on the contrary. They drew as close as they could to one another, and held each other's hands. They were maddened beyond endurance at not being able to come together, and they cursed the iron bars. But Lancelot boasted that if the Queen consented, he would enter the chamber; it was not the bars of the window that were preventing him. The Queen said, "Do you not see how solid these bars are—how could you break them, or even bend them…?"

"My lady," answered Lancelot, "do not think of that! The iron is worthless as far as I am concerned. Nothing will stop me from coming in to you, but you yourself. If you grant your permission, the way is free. But if you do not wish it, then the path is so full of obstacles that I shall never be able to pass."

"As for me, I desire it," said the Queen. "My wishes will never prevent you…"

...The knight prepared himself to attack the window. He grasped the bars, heaved and pulled them down until he had quickly bent them all and could force them out of their sockets. But the iron was so sharp that it pierced the tip of one finger to the bone, and sliced through another at the first joint. But his preoccupation was so intense that he felt no pain from these wounds, nor did he notice the blood which poured from them...The Queen stretched out her arms to him and embraced him; she pressed him to her breast, and then drew him into the bed beside her. She made him the most beautiful welcome that anyone could do who was inspired by love in their heart. Indeed, she felt for him great love, but Lancelot loved her a thousand times more. Love had taken root in his heart so completely, that there was scarcely any left over for other hearts. Now Lancelot had everything he desired; the queen wished him to stay beside her and enjoy her; he held her in his arms and she held him in hers. Their blows were so gentle, so sweet, that through their kisses and caresses they experienced a joy and wonder the equal of which has never been known or heard of. But I shall be silent on this subject, for it should never be recounted; for the rarest and most delectable pleasures are those which are hinted at, but never told.

CHRÉTIEN DE TROYES, *Lancelot*

Above: *Dante Gabriel Rossetti, "Arthur's Tomb." Rossetti has imagined the location of this final scene between the two lovers at Arthur's tomb; but his portrayal of Lancelot's eager intensity and Guinevere's sorrowful reluctance is brilliant, and very much in keeping with the medieval* Morte Arthur *and Malory's* Le Morte d'Arthur.

Taking his cue from some hints about Lancelot's early life given by Chrétien, the anonymous author of the prose Lancelot gives an enormously long account of his hero's childhood and his upbringing by the Lady of the Lake. At last, Lancelot comes to King Arthur's court to be knighted, where he sets eyes on Guinevere for the first time:

The queen looked at the young man closely, and he at her, whenever he could turn his eyes towards her without being noticed, and he marvelled at where such great beauty as he saw appear in her could come from. He considered the beauty of the Lady of the Lake, and of all other ladies he had ever seen before, as nothing in comparison with this. And he was not one bit wrong if he thought that no other woman came close to the queen, for she was the lady of

ladies and the fount of beauty; yet if he had known the great worth that was in her, he would have looked at her still more longingly, for there was no woman, rich or poor, of her outstanding qualities.

She asked Sir Yvain what the young man was called, and he replied that he did not know.

"But do you know," she went on, "whose son he is, and where he was born?"

"No, my lady," he replied, "except that I know he is from Gaul, for he often speaks in that language."

Then the queen took the young man by the hand, and asked him

Below: Julia Margaret Cameron persuaded friends to pose in costume for her photographic illustrations to Tennyson's Idylls of the King in 1874. This shows "The Parting of Sir Lancelot and Queen Guinevere."

Right: *Another composite illustration from the beautiful manuscript* Roman de Lancelot du Lac *(Pierpont Morgan Library, MS 805 f. 253 v). On the left, Lancelot has been given a magic chessboard, whose gold and silver pieces move of their own accord; Lancelot is the first person to win a game. In the centre, he sends the chessboard as a gift to Guinevere. On the right, Guinevere plays but loses.*

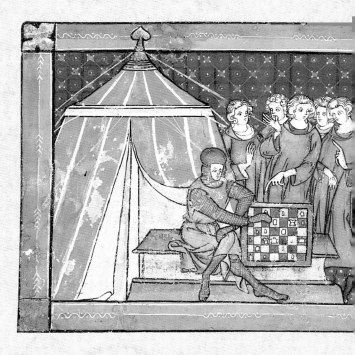

where he was from. And when he felt her touch, he trembled and started just as if he had woken up that moment, and he was thinking about her so intently that he did not hear what she said. And she realised that he was completely astounded, so she asked him once more, "Tell me where you are from." And he gazed at her innocently and said, sighing heavily, that he did not know. She asked him again what his name was; he said he had no idea. And now the queen realised that he was amazed and worried, but she did not dare to believe that it was on her account; yet all the same, she suspected a little that it was, and she left off talking for a while.

ANON, PROSE *Lancelot*

Lancelot goes on to perform great feats of knighthood in the next two years, purely in order to make a name for himself so that Guinevere will be impressed and look favourably on him. At last, by means of his friend Galehot, Lancelot meets and speaks with the queen. She questions him long and hard about his activities in order to find out the truth of his feelings. In this version of the relationship, Guinevere is clearly older and much more experienced than Lancelot in the ways of love, and she is always in control:

"And the other day, at the tourney, for what reason did you do such great deeds of arms?"

And he began to sigh very heavily. And the queen gave him no time to recover, for she knew very well how it was with him.

"You may tell me," she said, "in perfect security, for I shall never disclose your secret. I know very well that you have done this for the sake of some lady or some damsel. Now tell me who she is, by the faith you owe me."

"Ah, my lady!" he said, "I see that I shall have to tell you. Lady, it is you."

"I?" she said.

"Truly, my lady."

"Not for me did you break those three lances which my maiden brought you, for I deliberately left myself out of the message."

"Lady," he said, "for them I did what I should, and for you, what I could."

"Now tell me, all the deeds of chivalry that you have done, for whom did you do them?"

"For you, my lady."

"What?" she said, "do you love me so much?"

"My lady," he said, "I love no-one else, and not even myself, so much as I love you."

ANON, PROSE *Lancelot*

having brought out this confession, Guinevere proceeds to tease the young knight by refusing to believe him and claiming that he loves one of the other ladies who are sitting nearby. Lancelot is so distressed by this that he turns pale with grief and almost faints, upon which Galehot returns and pleads with Guinevere to grant Lancelot her love. She agrees to do this, as a token of her friendship for Galehot(!) and the bargain is sealed with a kiss, stolen under the very eyes of Guinevere's ladies-in-waiting by using Galehot's body as a shield:

"Thank you, my lady," said Galehot. "But now it is fitting for you to pay an advance against the agreement."

"You cannot suggest anything that I will not perform," said the queen.

"My lady, many thanks," said Galehot. "Therefore you must kiss him in front of me, as a commencement of your true love."

"In my opinion this is certainly neither the time nor the place for kissing, but do not doubt that I am just as willing and eager to do so as he is. But there are those ladies over there, who are wondering what we have been doing all this time, and they would

Opposite, above: An incomplete watercolour study for Dante Gabriel Rossetti's mural in the Oxford Union Debating Hall, illustrating Lancelot's dreamed vision of Guinevere.

Below: Guinevere places about the neck of Lancelot a magic shield sent to her by the Lady of the Lake. The Lady herself arrives and administers a healing ointment to Lancelot. (Pierpont Morgan Library, MS 805 f.109)

order, so she did not dare to oppose them. And then they took
this damsel here," he said indicating the queen, "who had called
herself Guinevere, and they put her in the bed in the place of my
lady, against whom this treason had been plotted. And then afterwards they came to Guinevere, and carried her out of the country and imprisoned her in an abbey where she has been in great
misery until now…"

Arthur is asked to take back the "true" queen or return her
dowry. The false Guinevere claims she is so confident of
her right that she has chosen the aged Berthelai to defend
her and as evidence a wedding-ring is produced, identical to Guinevere's.
Arthur seems to believe her story and a date is set for a trial by
combat while Gawain and the other knights support and comfort the
distressed Guinevere.

Meanwhile in Camelide, Berthelai tricks Arthur into hunting alone for a fictitious wild boar, whereupon he is captured by Berthelai's men. Berthelai and the damsel put a powerful love potion in Arthur's drink and he falls passionately in love with the damsel, although he feels remorse for abandoning his faithful wife and knights. After fifteen days of receiving the love potion, Arthur has been firmly convinced by the damsel's persuasiveness that she is the true queen and Guinevere has deceived him.

"But be sure," he said, "that I no longer believe that any lady in the world could be of avail to her who has so shamed me in this land through her cunning, and made me disloyal to my Creator, because of which I feel great anguish at heart. And yet no lady," said he, "has ever been so sensible as she is, nor so courteous, nor so sweet, nor so noble. And her bounty and largesse are greater

than in any queen before her, for she was so endowed with good qualities that through her great valour she has won the hearts of both rich and poor throughout the realm of Britain, so that they say she is the emerald of all ladies. But I believe," he said, "that she has done all this in order to deceive me and the others, so that no-one should perceive her treachery and her crimes."

"Sire," said the damsel, "it has always been the case that those who aspire to evil are more deceitful than other people."

"Truly," said the king, "it could well be. But I marvel greatly that a treacherous heart can be so endowed with such noble qualities as hers is. But nonetheless," said he, "I shall say no more for the love that I bear you, but I hate her with such great hatred that I shall never be happy as long as she has life in her body, for it will not fail to happen that she loses both body and soul."

Opposite: Lancelot rescues Guinevere from being burned at the stake, phase two: he puts her on his horse and rides away. Glorious illustration by N. C. Wyeth, The Boy's King Arthur, 1903.

rthur publicly acknowledges his belief in the damsel and sends a message to Gawain commanding him to lead his barons to Camelide to witness the crowning of the damsel as queen. Although overjoyed to hear Arthur is alive, Gawain is alarmed that he wishes Guinevere to be tried for treason. In her distressed state Guinevere sends for Galehot and Lancelot who respond at once:

"Lady," said Galehot, "do not distress yourself, but conduct yourself with assurance, lest it might seem that you are guilty of the treason of which you are accused. You should go with Sir Gawain, your nephew, and with the other good men who all love you and who would never willingly permit you to be harmed. And we shall go with you, Lancelot and I, and be sure that I shall strive with all my power in this business. And if they decide that there must be a battle, then it is already arranged who will fight on your behalf. And if they want to put you to death in some other way, we have a good enough company to be able to rescue you and take you away by force, and they will not dare to oppose us. And then," said Galehot, "I shall bring you into my country, and I shall give to you and to my friend here the kingdom of Soerlois, which is amply wealthy and beautiful; and he will be king, and you will be queen, and you will lead a good life together with people who thoroughly cherish you."

"Sir," she said, "my thanks for your promise. I shall not refuse this, for you are the man in the whole world in whom I have the greatest faith to save my honour and my life, after Lancelot here."

"Lady," said Galehot, "be sure that I shall protect you with all my might and I shall be on your side against all men, even if I must do harm to King Arthur, whose man I am."

Below: A composite illustration of the episode of the False Guinevere, from the Roman de Lancelot du Lac. On the left, Lancelot fights against the three successive champions of the False Guinevere. Two are lying battered and bloody on the ground as Lancelot polishes off the third. The False Guinevere and her mentor Bertholais are burned at the stake on the right. (Pierpont Morgan Library, MS 805/6 f. 119v)

Gawain and the other knights declare they will protect Guinevere and once the barons have arrived they set off for Camelide. The king is pleased to see the knights but has Guinevere imprisoned, though to Arthur's dismay, the knights insist on a fair trial. Galehot has sent for his own knights and comforts Guinevere by saying he will give his life for her. When both sides meet Arthur is hostile to Guinevere who, in turn, is mortified to see the damsel by Arthur's side. The king and the barons then withdraw to judge Guinevere—finally Arthur emerges and declares:

"My lords, you have heard how this damsel commanded me to take her back again as the woman I had married. And I want you to know that I have recognised her and I know truly that she is the one whom Leodegan gave me by the hand. Now we have judged that this Guinevere who is there must have her hair cut off, with the scalp, because she made herself queen and wore a

crown on her head that she should not have worn. And afterwards, she shall have the palms of her hands sliced off, because she was consecrated and anointed, as the hands of no woman ought to be unless a king has married her faithfully and properly in Holy Church. And then, she shall be dragged through this town, which is the chief city of this realm, because she has been held in such great honour by murder and by treason. And after all that, she shall be burned, and the ashes scattered, just as the news will run through all lands of the justice that shall have been done, and so that no-one will ever be so bold as to undertake such a business again. And therefore, because we know in truth that she is guilty and so that everyone must be a witness to it, we have decreed and judged that it is fitting that anyone who wishes to defend her from this charge of treason shall fight all alone against three knights, the best ones that this lady can find in this whole country."

ANON, PROSE *Lancelot*

awain and Kay leap to defend Guinevere, but Lancelot, inflamed by his love, insists on fighting the three knights. He tells Guinevere she has nothing to fear and she replies that she indeed has no fear because of her faith in her innocence and Lancelot's prowess—he duly earns her honour by winning the combat. Berthelai and the damsel confess their treachery before an angry and ashamed Arthur; they suffer the same fate meant for Guinevere. What is extraordinary about this account is Arthur's clear inclination, right from the first, to believe in the damsel in spite of his clear acknowledgement of Guinevere's great virtues. There is a sense in which Guinevere continues to be secure despite the dangerous lawsuit and the enmity of the king, because none of the knights believes the damsel's story and all are prepared to support Guinevere's cause. This is not the case in our final instance of Guinevere wrongly accused, which occurs toward the end of Le Morte d'Arthur. In Malory's translation, Guinevere has just had a huge quarrel with Lancelot, and in order to show that she "had as great joy in all other knights of the Round Table as she had in Sir Lancelot," she invites twenty-four knights to a splendid dinner in London. Among the knights is Sir Gawain, as well as his enemy Sir Pinel le Savage:

And so these four and twenty knights should dine with the queen in a privy place by themselves, and there was made a great feast of all manner of dainties. But Sir Gawain had a custom that he used daily at dinner and at supper, that he loved well all manner of fruit, and in especial apples and pears. And therefore whomsoever dined or feasted Sir Gawain would commonly purvey for good fruit for him, and so did the queen for to please Sir Gawain. For Sir Gawain was a passing hot knight by nature, and this Sir Pinel hated Sir Gawain because of his kinsman Sir Lamorak de Gales; and therefore for pure envy and hate Sir Pinel empoisoned certain apples for to poison Sir Gawain.

And so this was well until the end of the meat; and so it befell by misfortune a good knight named Sir Patrise, cousin unto Sir Mador de la Porte, to take a poisoned apple. And after he had eaten it, he swelled so til he burst, and there Sir Patrise fell down suddenly dead along them. Then every knight leapt from the board ashamed, and enraged with wrath, nigh out of their wits. For they knew not what to say; considering Queen Guinevere made the feast and the dinner, they all had suspicion unto her.

"My lady, the queen," said Sir Gawain, "wit you well, madam, that this dinner was made for me, for all folks that know my condition understand that I love well fruit, and now I see well

I had near been slain; therefore, madam, I dread me lest you will be shamed."

Then the queen stood still and was sore abashed, that she knew not what to say.

"This shall not so be ended," said Sir Mador de la Porte, "for here have I lost a full noble knight of my blood; and therefore upon this shame and despite I will be revenged to the utterance." And there openly Sir Mador accused the queen of the death of his cousin, Sir Patrise.

Then stood they all still, that none would speak a word against him, for they all had great suspicion unto the queen because she let make that dinner. And the queen was so abashed that she could do no other, but wept so heartily that she fell into a swoon. With this noise and cry came to them King Arthur, and when he knew of that trouble he was a passing heavy man.

MALORY, *Le Morte d'Arthur*

Sir Mador accuses the queen of treason and Arthur bids him not to be so hasty as a brave knight will undoubtedly defend her—however none of the knights believes she is innocent. Guinevere seems in much greater danger here, having banished from court the only man who would take her part in right or in wrong, and when all the knights including Gawain believe her to be guilty. Fortunately, of course, Lancelot turns up at the eleventh hour to fight on her behalf and she is saved from an ignominious death.

Left: *King Arthur imprisoned in a tower by the False Guinevere and about to fall victim to her deceitful charms. (Bodleian Library, MS Rawlinson Q.b.6 f.123 v)*

Guinevere the Jealous Harpy

Parallel to the descriptions of Guinevere as a noble lady was from an early date a strong tradition of a bad Guinevere. This is a queen whom power has corrupted and she uses her feminine wiles to manipulate Arthur, throwing tantrums, crying or sulking to get her own way. Portrayals of her love-affair with Lancelot here show that she is capable of extreme jealousy and, worst of all, she does not flinch at scheming to harm those who have thwarted her desires out of spite.

The first occasion on which we meet this Guinevere is in one of the twelfth-century Breton lays of Marie de France, "Lanval." Here Lanval, a very good-natured and noble but sadly impoverished knight, has had the good fortune to become the lover of a beautiful and wealthy fairy mistress. But there is a condition attached to her love—he must never speak of her to a single soul. If he is discreet, he can enjoy her wealth and her person as long as he likes; but if he reveals her existence to anyone, she will never see him again. Lanval returns to Arthur's court and becomes very popular through his new generosity. He catches the wandering eye of Queen Guinevere:

When the queen saw Lanval go in, she made her way directly to him. She sat down, called him over, and revealed all her heart to him: "Lanval, I have honoured you much, and have greatly cherished and loved you. You can enjoy all my love; just tell me your desires! I grant you my love—you should be glad of such a gift."

"Lady," he replied, "please allow me to leave! I have no intention of loving you. I have served the king for a long time, and I do not want to break faith with him. Not for you nor for your love will I do wrong to my liege lord."

The queen became furiously angry, enraged at being spoken to like this. "Lanval," she said, "I know perfectly well that you don't care much for the delights of love; people have told me often enough that you have no interest in women. You have been well-taught, you and those friends you amuse yourself with. Shameful wicked traitors—my lord is greatly abused, to have suffered you to be close to him; in my opinion, he may lose his soul for it!"

When he heard this, he was bitterly hurt; nor was he slow to respond. He said such things, by ill luck, as he would often have

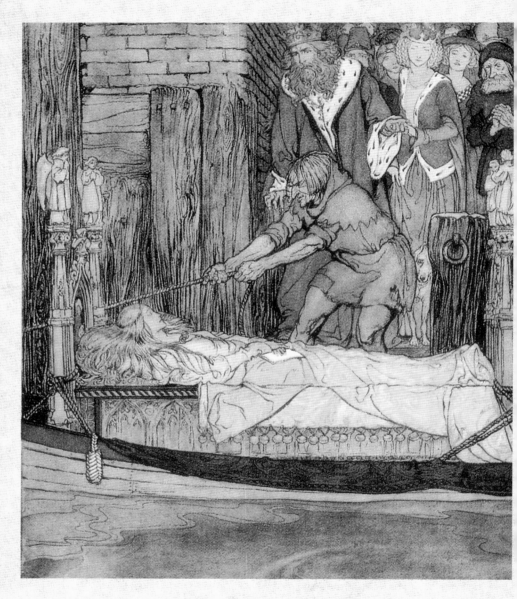

cause to regret. "Lady," he said, "I have absolutely nothing to do with people of that calling; but I am in love, and I am loved in return, by one who would certainly take the prize over all other ladies I know. And I will tell you one thing you can be sure of: one of the damsels who serve her, even the poorest maid, is better than you, my lady queen, in figure, in face, and in beauty, as well as upbringing and bounty."

The queen fled away at once, and went weeping to her chamber. She was very sullen and angry, because of the way he had so vilified her. She lay sickened upon her bed; never, she said, would she rise again, unless the king did her justice for the wrong she complained of.

The king had repaired to the woods, and the day had given him much pleasure. He entered the queen's chambers. When she saw him she cried out and fell at his feet. She begged him to have pity on her, and she told him that Lanval had shamed her. He had demanded her love and then, because she had refused him, he had grossly insulted and reviled her; he had boasted of a lover who was so exquisite, so noble, so proud, that even the meanest of the chambermaids who served her was more worthy than the queen. The king was violently enraged, and he swore a great oath: that Lanval could defend himself in court against this charge, he would have him either burned or hanged. The king came out of the chamber and summoned three of his barons. He sent them to fetch Lanval, who...had returned to his lodgings. He fully realised that he had lost his beloved; for he had revealed their love. He was all alone,...heavy and grief-stricken. He often called aloud upon his love, but she cared nothing for him. He sighed and wept and lamented, and from time to time he swooned; then he would beg his beloved a hundred times, to speak to her lover. He cursed his heart and his mouth; it was a marvel that he did not kill himself...

The men the king sent for came, and told Lanval that he must go to court without delay: the king had commanded him through them, because the queen had accused him. Lanval went, with great sorrow; he would willingly be killed. He came before the king in great grief, silent and mute, showing the appearance of unbearable sorrow. The king said to him angrily: "Vassal, you have greatly wronged me! You began a foul undertaking, to dishonour and revile me, and vilify the queen. You have made a foolish boast: that your beloved is too noble to be true, when even her handmaiden is more beautiful and more worthy than the queen." Lanval denied the accusation of having dishonoured and shamed his lord, word for word, as the king had spoken it, insofar as he had sought the queen's love, and he told how he himself had rejected the queen's advances; but what he had said of the love he had boasted about, he admitted the truth; but he had lost her, to his sorrow. As for that part of the charge, he told them that he would do whatever the court decided.

MARIE DE FRANCE, *"Lanval"*

Opposite: *"How King Arthur and Queen Guinevere Went to See the Barge that Bore the Corpse of Elaine the Fair Maiden of Astolat."* Watercolour by Arthur Rackham, The Romance of King Arthur, 1917.

rthur charges the barons to sit in judgment of Lanval, and a date is set for the verdict. The majority are in sympathy with the accused, and beg him to produce his mistress in order to prove that he did not make his claim in malice. Lanval explains that this is now impossible and the court regrettably appears to have no excuse for delivering a verdict other than that demanded by the king, nor to delay further. At this pitch of suspense, with the king and queen baying for Lanval's blood and a sympathetic court unable to help him if he can't prove the truth of his claim about his lady, the fairy mistress decides to relent and save him.

First two maidens arrive, ravishingly lovely, to ask the king for lodgings for their mistress. Two more maidens follow, even more beautiful, but still not Lanval's lover. The king presses the judges again for a verdict, "...that they should render their judgement: they had already drawn out the process too long, and the queen was becoming very angry at having to wait such a long time for their decision." Finally the damsel herself arrives, and there is a long description of her dazzling beauty. She mounts the dais and strips down to her shift so that everyone can appreciate her charms. She speaks to Arthur:

"Lord king, I have loved one of your vassals: see him there! It is Lanval. He has been accused in your court, and I no longer want things to turn out badly for him. As for what he said, you will decide whether or not he did wrong to the queen by that: but he certainly never requested her love. Of the boast that he made, if through me he can be acquitted, let your barons declare him free!" The king granted that the judges should exercise their judgement. There was not one of them who did not judge that Lanval was entirely justified.

MARIE DE FRANCE, "Lanval"

nfortunately the text does not record Guinevere's reaction to this public humiliation. Malory's Guinevere in Le Morte d'Arthur is a complex person, suffering violent pangs of jealousy whenever she suspects that Lancelot has been conducting love-affairs with other women. On one occasion Lancelot has actually been with another woman—Elaine, the daughter of King Pelles of Corbenic and the mother of Lancelot's son, Galahad. Lancelot was induced to sleep with Elaine because he had been given a drug which made him think she was Guinevere:

So the noise sprang in Arthur's court that Lancelot had gotten a child upon Elaine, the daughter of King Pelles, wherefore Queen Guinevere was wroth, and gave many rebukes to Sir

Lancelot, and called him false knight. And then Sir Lancelot told the queen all, and how he was made to lie by her in likeness of the queen. So the queen held Sir Lancelot excused. And as the book saith, King Arthur had been in France, and had made war upon the mighty king Claudas, and had won much of his lands. And when the king was come again he let cry a great feast, that all lords and ladies of all England should be there….

laine hears of the feast, her father grants her leave to attend and following his advice, she spares no expense to look her finest. Her natural beauty and the richness of her retinue win the praise of all at Arthur's court—except that of Lancelot, who shuns her in his shame over their previous affair, while admitting to himself that she is the fairest woman at court.

Lancelot, of course, is the one person whom Elaine desires. Her wily handmaiden, Dame Brisen, arranges to pretend to be Guinevere's servant and to lead Lancelot to Elaine's bed, not the queen's. A medieval comedy of errors follows, as Guinevere, fearing double foul play, has installed Elaine in a chamber adjacent to her own:

Then the queen sent for Sir Lancelot and bade him come to her chamber that night: "Or else I am sure," said the queen, "that ye will go to your lady's bed, Dame Elaine, by whom ye gat Galahad."

"Ah, madam," said Sir Lancelot, "never say ye so, for that I did was against my will."

"Then," said the queen, "look that ye come to me when I send for you."

"Madam," said Lancelot, "I shall not fail you, but I shall be ready at your commandment."…

So when time came that all folks were abed, Dame Brisen came to Sir Lancelot's bedside and said, "Sir Lancelot du Lake, sleep you? My lady, Queen Guinevere, lieth and awaiteth upon you."

"O my fair lady," said Sir Lancelot, "I am ready to go with you where you will have me."

So Sir Lancelot threw upon him a long gown, and his sword in his hand; and then Dame Brisen took him by the finger and led him to her lady's bed, Dame Elaine: and then she departed and left them in bed together. Wit you well the lady was glad, and so was Sir Lancelot, for he weened that he had had another in his arms. Now we leave them kissing and clipping, as was natural thing; and now speak we of Queen Guinevere that sent one of her women unto Sir Lancelot's bed; and when she came there she found the bed cold, and he was away; so she came to the queen and told her all.

"Alas," said the queen, "where is that false knight become?"
Then the queen was nigh out of her wit, and then she writhed
and weltered as a mad woman, and might not sleep a four or
five hours.

L ancelot's unfortunate habits of snoring and talking in his sleep
alert the insomniac Guinevere to his presence in the next
chamber to hers—Elaine's! The distressed queen coughs
loudly enough to awaken the noisy knight:

73

And then he knew well that he lay not by the queen; and therewith he leapt out of his bed as he had been a madman, in his shirt, and the queen met him in the floor; and thus she said: "False traitor knight that thou art, look thou never abide in my court, and avoid my chamber, and not so hardy, thou false traitor knight that thou art, that ever thou come in my sight!"

"Alas," said Sir Lancelot; and therewith he took such an heartly sorrow at her words that he fell down to the floor in a swoon. And therewithal Queen Guinevere departed. And when Sir Lancelot woke out of his swoon, he leapt out at a bay window into a garden, and there with thorns he was all to-cratched in his visage and his body: and so he ran forth he wist not whither, and was wild man as ever was man; and so he ran two year, and never man might have grace to know him…

When Dame Elaine heard the queen so to rebuke Sir Lancelot,…she said unto Queen Guinevere, "Madam, ye are greatly to blame for Sir Lancelot, for now ye have lost him, for I saw and heard by his countenance that he is mad for ever."…

"Dame Elaine," said the queen, "when it is daylight I charge you and command you to avoid my court; and for the love ye owe

Right: *Lancelot descends into madness when he is reviled by Queen Guinevere for accidentally sleeping with Elaine of Corbenic. (Bodleian Library, Oxford, MS Rawl Q.b.6 f.92v)*

unto Sir Lancelot discover not his counsel, for and ye do, it will be his death."

"As for that," said Dame Elaine, "I dare undertake he is marred for ever, and that have ye made; for ye nor I are like to rejoice him, for he made the most piteous groans when he leapt out yonder bay window that ever I heard man make. Alas," said fair Elaine, and "Alas," said the Queen Guinevere, "for now I wot well we have lost him forever."

Elaine leaves in the morning, after telling Lancelot's cousin, Sir Bors, of the whole affair. He rebukes Guinevere, who begs him to find Lancelot. Only after two years of wandering as a madman is Lancelot found in the grounds of Corbenic by Elaine, and healed by the Holy Grail. He feels unable to return to Camelot because of Guinevere's ban, so he goes to live in a nearby castle with Elaine and his son; but his heart is full of grief. Eventually he is discovered by the other members of his family, who bring him back, with much rejoicing, to Camelot, where Guinevere is so happy to see him alive and sane that she forgets the incident with Elaine and lifts the exile, welcoming him back to court.

Later in the cycle, Lancelot's passion for Guinevere causes him to neglect the quest for the Holy Grail, however his alleged (but this time not true) dalliance with other ladies causes her to make another scene:

So befell that Sir Lancelot had many resorts of ladies and damosels that daily resorted unto him, that besought him to be their champion, and in all such matters of right Sir Lancelot applied him daily for to do for the pleasure of Our Lord, Jesu Christ. And ever as much as he might he withdrew him from the company and fellowship of Queen Guinevere, for to eschew the slander and the noise; wherefore the queen waxed wroth with Sir Lancelot. And upon a day she called Sir Lancelot into her chamber, and said thus:

"Sir Lancelot, I see and feel daily that thy love beginneth to slake, for thou hast no joy to be in my presence, but ever thou art out of this court, and quarrels and matters thou hast nowadays for ladies and gentlewomen more than ever thou were wont to have aforehand."

Lancelot explains that he is trying to deflect the attention of vigilant members of the court from his relationship with Guinevere. He also maintains that he has Guinevere's welfare at heart as he fears their love-affair will put her in danger of reprisals from jealous knights and cause her great shame:

"And wit ye well, madam, the boldness of you and me will put us to great shame and slander; and that were me loath to see you dishonoured. And that is the cause I take upon me more for to do for damosels and maidens than ever I did tofore, that men should understand my joy and my delight is my pleasure to have ado for damosels and maidens."

All this while the queen stood still and let Sir Lancelot say what he would. And when he had all said she brast out on weeping, and so she sobbed and wept a great while. And when she might speak she said, "Lancelot, now I well understand that thou art a false recreant knight and a common lecher, and lovest and holdest other ladies, and by me thou hast disdain and scorn. For wit thou well," she said, "now I understand thy falsehood, and therefore shall I never love thee no more. And never be thou so hardy to come in my sight; and right here I discharge thee this court, that thou never come within it; and I forfend thee my fellowship, and upon pain of thy head that thou see me no more."

A little later, Lancelot decides to wear the favour of the young and beautiful Elaine of Astolat at a tournament, something he had never done before, because he wants to go in disguise and be sure that no-one will know who he is. At the tournament, he fights marvellously, but is severely wounded. Gawain accidentally discovers the identity of the mysterious knight, and carries the tale back to Camelot.

But when Queen Guinevere wist than Sir Lancelot bare the red sleeve of the Fair Maiden of Astolat she was nigh out of her mind for wrath. And then she sent for Sir Bors de Ganis in all the haste that might be. So when Sir Bors was come tofore the queen, then she said, "Ah Sir Bors, have ye heard how falsely Sir Lancelot hath betrayed me?"

"Alas madam," said Sir Bors, "I am afeared he hath betrayed himself and us all."

"No force," said the queen, "though he be destroyed, for he is a false traitor knight."

"Madam," said Sir Bors, "I pray you say ye not so, for wit you well I may not hear such language of him."

"Why Sir Bors," say she, "should I not call him traitor when he bare the red sleeve upon his head at Winchester, at the great jousts?"

"Madam," said Sir Bors, "that sleeve-bearing repenteth me sore, but I dare say he did it to none evil intent, but for this cause he bare the red sleeve that none of his blood should know him. For

Left: *Weakened by grief and fasting, Sir Lancelot swoons over the tomb of King Arthur and Queen Guinevere, crying, "My heart would not serve to sustain my careful body." A fine drawing by Walter Crane, 1904.*

or then we nor none of us all never knew that ever he bare token or sign of maid, lady ne gentlewoman."

"Fie on him!" said the queen, "Yet for all his pride and bobaunce there ye proved yourself his better."

"Nay madam, say ye never more so, for he beat me and my fellows, and might have slain us and he had would."

"Fie on him," said the queen, "for I heard Sir Gawain say before my lord Arthur that it were marvel to tell the great love that is between the Fair Maiden of Astolat and him." I dare say, as for my lord, Sir Lancelot, that he loveth no lady, gentlewoman, nor maid, but all he loveth in like much. And therefore madam," said Sir Bors, "ye may say what ye will, but wit ye well I will haste me to seek him, and find him wheresoever he be, and God send my good tidings of him."

Elaine of Astolat nurses Lancelot back to health and falls passionately in love with him. He rejects her love and returns to court; she dies and is put into a barge and taken to Westminster, where the sad tale of her unrequited love is made known to everyone by means of a letter addressed to Sir Lancelot and held in her dead hand.

Sir Lancelot is sent for and, on hearing her last words in the letter, laments her death. He declares that he did not willingly cause her death but feels somewhat to blame as her great love for him caused this tragedy:

"Ye might have showed her," said the queen, "some bounty and gentleness that might have preserved her life."

"Madam," said Sir Lancelot, "she would none other ways be answered but that she would be my wife, other else my paramour; and of these two I would not grant her, but I proffered her, for her good love that she showed me, a thousand pound yearly to her, and to her heirs, and to wed any manner knight that she could find best to love in her heart. For madam," said Sir Lancelot, "I love not to be constrained to love; for love must arise of the heart, and not by no constraint."

[The Fair Maiden is buried and Lancelot offers her mass-penny.]

Then the queen sent for Sir Lancelot, and prayed him of mercy, for why that she had been wroth with him causeless.

"This is not the first time," said Sir Lancelot, "that ye had been displeased with me causeless, but madam, ever I must suffer you, but what sorrow I endure I take no force."

MALORY, *Le Morte d'Arthur*

Tennyson, *relating this same episode, describes Guinevere's agony at the news of Lancelot's supposed infidelity more graphically. Arthur himself reports the outcome of the tournament to her:*

"Ill news, my Queen, for all who love him, this!—
His kith and kin, not knowing, set upon him;
So that he went sore wounded from the field:
Yet good news too: for goodly hopes are mine
That Lancelot is no more a lonely heart.
He wore, against his wont, upon his helm
A sleeve of scarlet, broider'd with great pearls,
Some gentle maiden's gift."

        "Yea, lord," she said,
"Thy hopes are mine," and saying that, she choked,
And sharply turned about to hide her face,
Past to her chamber, and there flung herself

Down on the great King's couch, and writhed upon it,
And clenched her fingers til they bit the palm,
And shriek'd out, "Traitor!" to the unhearing wall,
Then flash'd into wild tears, and rose again,
And moved about her palace, pale and proud."

*Later, Gawain brings back the news that Lancelot is loved by,
and as he believes, loves the Fair Maid of Astolat:*

So ran the tale like fire about the court,
Fire in a dry stubble a nine-days' wonder flared;
Till ev'n the knights at banquet twice or thrice
Forgot to drink to Lancelot and the Queen,
And pledging Lancelot and the lily maid,
Smiled at each other, while the Queen, who sat
With lips severely placid, felt the knot
Climb in her throat, and with her feet unseen
Crushed the wild passion out against the floor
Beneath the banquet, where the meats became
As wormwood, and she hated all who pledged.

TENNYSON, *Idylls of the King*

Left: *A superb depiction
of irresistible passion, dark
and bestial—Arthur
Rackham's watercolour
"How Sir Tristram and
Isoud Drank the Love
Drink,"* The Romance of
King Arthur, *1917.
Guinevere supported their
illicit love, and offered
them shelter in her court
when they had been exiled
from Cornwall.*

Guinevere Noble in Adversity

Opposite: *Guinevere watches from a balcony as Sir Galahad, Lancelot's son by Elaine of Corbenic, draws the sword from the stone, thus showing himself to be the knight predestined to achieve the Quest of the Holy Grail. From a north Italian manuscript of the late fourteenth century. (Bibliothèque Nationale, Paris, MS Fr. 343 f. 4)*

Although Queen Guinevere may be portrayed unsympathetically at other times, there are many occasions where she exhibits true dignity and strength. If the real test of character lies in how a person handles catastrophe, then Guinevere triumphs. It is in the face of imminent disaster that the queen's innate nobility emerges, whether she be bravely confronting an enemy endangering the lives of her knights or resolutely facing the consequences when her love-affair with Lancelot is exposed.

One example of such admirable dignity occurs when, even in the midst of her agonizing jealousy of Elaine of Corbenic, she can find it in her heart to say nothing but good of the son her hated rival has borne to Lancelot:

Then the king, at the queen's request, made [Galahad] to alight and to unlace his helm, that the queen might see him in the visage. When she beheld him she said, "Soothly I dare well say that Sir Lancelot begat him, for never two men resembled more in likeness, therefore it is no marvel though he be of great prowess."

So a lady that stood by the queen said, "Madam, for God's sake, ought he of right to be so good a knight?"

"Yea, forsooth," said the queen, "for he is of all parties come of the best knights of the world and of the highest lineage; for Sir Lancelot is come but of the eighth degree from Our Lord Jesu Christ, and Sir Galahad is of the ninth degree from Our Lord Jesu Christ, therefore I dare say they be the greatest gentlemen of the world."

MALORY, *Le Morte d'Arthur*

Malory's version of Guinevere's abduction by Meleagant also shows her behaving like a true heroine. Fearless for herself, she is more concerned to save the lives of her men. In a typically cowardly and treacherous fashion Meleagant has surrounded the queen and her ten unarmed knights (that is to say, they had swords but no armour) while they are out maying in the woods and fields beside Westminster:

So as the queen had Mayed and all her knights, all were bedashed with herbs, mosses and flowers, in the best manner and freshest.

Right so came out of a wood Sir Meliagaunt with an eight score men well harnessed, as they should fight in a battle, and bad the queen and her knights stand still, for despite their heads they would make them stand.

"Traitor knight," said Queen Guinevere, "what cast thou for to do? Wilt thou shame thyself? Bethink thee how thou art a king's son, and knight of the Table Round, and thou to be about to dishonour the noble king that made thee knight; thou shamest all knighthood and thyself, and me I let thee know thou shalt never shame, for I had rather cut mine own throat in twain rather than thou shouldest dishonour me."

"As for all this language," said Meliagaunt, "be it as it may, for wit you well, madam, I have loved you many a year, and never before now could I get you at such an advantage as I do now, and therefore I will take you as I find you."

Despite their woeful lack of armour, the ten noble knights declare they will fight to the death for their queen and a dreadful battle ensues. Although the knights succeed in slaying forty of Meleagant's best men, they are all severely wounded:

So when the queen saw her knights thus dolefully wounded, and needs must be slain at the last, then for pity and sorrow she cried out to Sir Meliagaunt, "Slay not my noble knights, and I will go with thee upon this covenant, that thou save them, and suffer them not to be hurt more, with this, that they be led with me wheresoever thou leadest me, for I will rather slay myself than I will go with thee, unless these my noble knights may be in my presence."

"Madam," said Meliagaunt, "for your sake they shall be led with you into mine own castle, with that you will be ruled, and ride with me."

Guinevere's finest hour, however, is undoubtedly the terrible moment when she and Lancelot are discovered together in her bedchamber by Sir Mordred and his co-conspirators:

But thus as the queen and Lancelot were together, there came Sir Agravain and Sir Mordred, with twelve knights with them of the Round Table, and they said with crying voice, "Traitor knight, Sir Lancelot du Lake, now art thou taken."

And thus they cried with a loud voice, that all the court might hear it; and they all fourteen were armed at all points as they should fight in a battle.

Opposite: *"Queen Guinevere Maying" by John Collier (1850–1934). An aloof and mystical queen conscious of her role in a rite, not merely enjoying a pastime.*

"Alas," said Queen Guinevere, "now are we mischieved both."

"Madam," said Sir Lancelot, "is there here any armour within your chamber, that I might cover my body withal? And if there be any, give it me, and I shall soon stop their malice, by the grace of God."

"Truly," said the queen, "I have none armour, shield, sword, nor spear; wherefore I dread me sore our long love is come to a mischievous end, for I hear by their noise there be many noble knights, and well I believe they are surely armed; against them you may make no resistance. Wherefore you are likely to be slain, and then I shall be burnt. For if you might escape them," said the queen, "I would not doubt but that you would rescue me in what danger that ever I stood in."

"Alas," said Sir Lancelot, "in all my life thus was I never bestad, that I should be thus shamefully slain for lack of mine armour."

But ever as one Sir Agravain and Sir Mordred cried, "Traitor knight, come out of the queen's chamber, for wit thou well, thou art so beset that thou shalt not escape."

"O Jesu mercy," said Sir Lancelot, "this shameful cry and noise I may not suffer, for better were death at once than thus to endure this pain."

Then he took the queen in his arms, and kissed her, and said, "Most noble Christian queen, I beseech you as you have ever been my special good lady, and I at all times your true poor knight unto my power, and as I never failed you in right nor in wrong, sithen the first day King Arthur made me knight, that you will pray for my soul if that I be here slain, for well I am assured that Sir Bors, mine nephew, and all the remnant of my kin, with Sir Lavaine and Sir Urry, that they will not fail you to rescue you from the fire; and therefore, mine own lady, recomfort yourself, whatsoever becomes of me, that you go with Sir Bors, my nephew, and Sir Urry, and they all will do you all the pleasure that they can or may, that you shall live like a queen upon my lands."

"Nay, Lancelot," said the queen, "wit thou well, I will never live after thy days, but if thou be slain I will take my death as meekly for Jesus Christ's sake as ever did any Christian queen."

"Well, madam," said Lancelot, "since it is so that the day is come that our love must depart, wit you well I shall sell my life as dear as I may; and a thousandfold," said Sir Lancelot, "I am more heavier for you than for myself. And now I had lever be lord of all Christendom, that I had sure armour upon me, that men might speak of my deeds or ever I were slain."

"Truly," said the queen, "I wish, if it might please God, that they would take me and slay me, and suffer you to escape."

Opposite: *This rare painting by William Morris in the Tate Gallery is usually known as "Guinevere," though it is sometimes called "Iseult." The rumpled bedclothes, her unclasped girdle, and preoccupied expression hint at seething sexual guilt.*

"That shall never be," said Sir Lancelot, "God defend me from such a shame, but Jesu be thou my shield and mine armour!"

MALORY, *Le Morte d'Arthur*

Malory has here amplified the same scene between Lancelot and Guinevere from his source, the French Mort Artu. Here Guinevere tells Lancelot:

"Fair sweet friend, we are betrayed."

"What, my lady?" said he, "what is it?"

Then he listened and he heard at the door a loud noise from the men who were trying to break open the door by force, but they could not.

"Ah! Fair sweet friend," said the queen, "now we are shamed and slain; now the king will know about you and me. This tangle has been wrought by Agravain."

"Indeed," said Lancelot, "do not concern yourself, my lady; he has only brought about his own death, for he will be the first one to die."

Then they both leapt out of the bed and dressed themselves as best they could.

"Ha! Lady," said Lancelot, "Do you have here a hauberk, or any other armour with which to protect my body?"

"Truly," said the queen, "nothing at all; for our misfortune is so great that it will be the death of us, both you and me. And this grieves me, so God help me, much more for your sake than for my own, because your death will be a much greater loss than mine. But notwithstanding, if God would only grant that you should escape from this place whole and well, I know well that there is no-one yet born who would dare deliver me up to death for this misdeed, while he knew you to be alive."

ANON, *Mort Artu*

The queen then orders Lancelot to go as soon as he can safely do so, even though without him there she will be defenceless against her detractors. Typically, Malory transferred the remark about being more concerned for Lancelot's safety than for her own from Guinevere to Lancelot. He was generally more interested in the heroic character of Lancelot and tried consistently to make him appear to advantage even when his French sources were critical. For Malory, the supreme quality is loyalty. At the end of his story he gives to Guinevere the ultimate accolade, that "ever while she lived she was a true lover, and therefore she had a good end."

Opposite: "Queen Guinevere's Moonlight Ride to Almesbury," engraving by Gustav Doré.

Left: Eleanor F. Brockdale's conventionally romantic version of the repentant Guinevere as a nun at Almesbury.

Opposite: *Sir Lancelot, summoned to Almesbury by a dream, arrives to find Guinevere's dead body. N. C. Wyeth* The Boy's King Arthur *1927.*

When Sir Lancelot was brought to her, then she said to all the ladies, "Through this man and me hath all this war been wrought, and the death of the noblest knights of the world; for through our love that we have loved together is my most noble lord slain. Therefore Sir Lancelot, know that I am set to get my soul's health…and therefore I require thee and beseech thee heartily, for all the love that ever was betwixt us, that thou never see me more in the visage; and I command thee, on God's behalf, that thou forsake my company…for through thee and me is the flower of kings and knights destroyed; therefore, Sir Lancelot, go to thy realm, and there take thee a wife, and live with her in joy and bliss; and I pray thee heartily, pray for me to Our Lord, that I may amend my misliving."

"Now, sweet madam," said Sir Lancelot, "would you that I should turn again to my country and there wed a lady? No, Madam, that shall I never do, for I shall never be so false to you of that I have promised; but the same destiny that you have taken you to, I will take unto me, to please Jesu…for I take record of God, in you I have had earthly joy. But since I find you thus disposed, I ensure you faithfully, I will ever take me to penance, and pray while my life lasts, if I may find any hermit, either gray or white, that will receive me. Wherefore, madam, I pray you kiss me and never no more."

"Nay," said the queen, "that shall I never do, but abstain me from such works." And they departed; but there was never so hard an hearted man but he would have wept to see the dolour that they made; for there was lamentation as they had been stungen with spears; and many times they swooned, and the ladies bare the queen to her chamber. And Sir Lancelot awoke, and went and took his horse, and rode all that day and all night in a forest, weeping.

MALORY, *Le Morte d'Arthur*

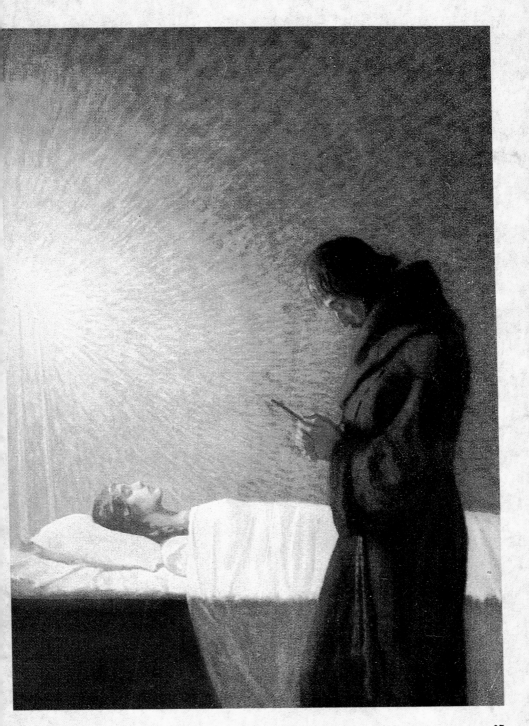

Glossary

Glossary

ado (have ado with): get involved with

alms-deeds: charitable deeds

bedash: sprinkle

bestad: beset, in a difficult position

bobaunce: pride, boastfulness

bounty: goodness, generosity

brast: burst

careful: sorrowful

cere-cloth: waxed cloth

clipping: embracing

covertly: secretly

dolour: grief

empoison: poison

ensample: example

forfend: forbid

garnished: furnished, provided

hardy: bold

hauberk: mail coat

lever: rather

lief: dear

loth: reluctant

mass-penny: offering at mass for the dead

Maying: observing the rite of May

noblesse: nobility, virtue

ordain: arrange

palfrey: a lady's riding horse

paramour: lover

passing: very

purvey: provide

recreant: coward

Sangreal/Sangrail: contraction of Old French "Sant Graal", the Holy Grail

sithen: since

slake: slacken, fade

utterance: utmost

victual: food

visage: face

waxed: grew

weened: believed, thought

wist: knew

wit: know (2nd person)

wont: accustomed

wot: know (1st person)

wroth: angry

Acknowledgements

The publisher would like to thank Charles Ziga for designing this book; Caroline Earle for editing; Gillian Speeth for assisting with picture research; Emily Head for preparing the index; Chris Berlingo; Gail Janensch. Grateful acknowledgement is also due to the following institutions for supplying the illustrations listed below with their page numbers:

Ashmolean Museum, Oxford: 52 (top); **The Bettmann Archive:** 7; **Bibliothèque Royale Albert Ier, Brussels:** 15; **Bibliothèque Nationale, Paris:** 27, 36, 58–9, 73, 81; **The Bodleian Library, Oxford:** 1 (MS Douce 383 f.14r), 65 (MS Rawlinson Q.b.6 f.123v), 74 (MS Rawlinson Q.b.6 f.92v); **The Bridgeman Art Library, London:** 11; **Bridgeman/Art Resource, New York:** 16–17, 82; Courtesy of the **British Tourist Authority:** 25; **Historic Scotland, Ancient Monuments Division:** 8; **Mary Evans Picture Library:** 18, 21, 40, 45, 54, 60, 67, 89, 90, 91, 93; **Museo de Arte de Ponce, Puerto Rico, Luis A. Ferre Foundation, Inc:** 12–13; **National Gallery of Scotland:** 4; **Pierpont Morgan Library/Art Resource, New York:** 22–3, 28–9, 30–1, 46–7, 50–1, 52–3, 62–3; Garrett Collection of Medieval and Renaissance Manuscripts, Manuscripts Division, Department of Rare Books and Special Collections, **Princeton University Libraries:** 33; **Tate Gallery London/Art Resource, New York:** 2 (and 87), 48.